DEDICATION

to my big sister Bri

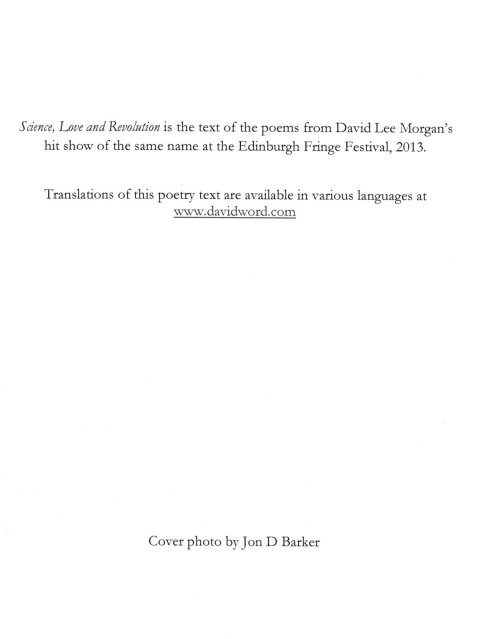

Science, Love and Revolution is the text of the poems from David Lee Morgan's hit show of the same name at the Edinburgh Fringe Festival, 2013.

Translations of this poetry text are available in various languages at
www.davidword.com

Cover photo by Jon D Barker

Science, Love and

Revolution

David Lee Morgan

CONTENTS

TIGER TALE

I had a dream where the tiger and I stood side by side

And the air was alive with the music of our beating hearts

This is my tiger, I said. Isn't she beautiful

Her teeth cut like diamonds, but they shine like stars

Then the tiger purred, the purr became a growl

The growl became a word, the time to dance is... now!

WORD

[*primate animal sounds*]

HAND!

hunh, ha, hey, ho
eh, ih, ah, ew
eee, ay, iy, oh
TOOL!

pah, buh, duh,
tig, ga, nuh,
kuh, juh, le,
suh, muh, chuh
r-r-r-r-r-ragh, zuh, vuh
FIRE!

[*laughter*]

WORD!

mother banana berry beetle grub yam
sister uncle brother father cousin kin clan

impala monkey cheetah catfish

bow and arrow hook and line

hunger death desire

dance dream moon wind

wolf enemy dog friend

animal-fur obsidian seashell

river lake ocean

barter boat wheel

sickle dam plough

millet rice maize

water-canal

goat horse cattle cow

priest king city wall

prison slave wife

road army empire

ritual sacrifice

planet alphabet tablet scroll

number circle triangle star

festival temple diamond gold

paper money poetry war

castle kingdom pilgrim pope

nativity communion jihad hijra

lord and lady serf and outlaw

carnival cathedral catapult crusade

compass telescope sextant astrolabe

buccaneer sugar-cane cotton-gin slave-trade

printing-press protest guillotine barricade

factory foundry model-t monopoly
gasoline caffeine telephone saxophone
black-hole rock 'n' roll blue-suede free-trade
concrete wall-street war-crime picket-line
colony corporation contraception insurrection

hospital popsicle methadone chromosome
pizzeria gonorrhea nagasaki hiroshima
penicillin television auschwitz crucifix
lipstick dayshift weblog gulag hot-dog kalashnikov
microchip paperclip spaceship cheese-dip

blood brain demon idea
mud angel reason ikea
love anger grief absolution
vaccination air-pollution
education evolution
inspiration revolution
danger freedom
building breeding

without a *we are*, there is no *i am*
the river was a god until we built a dam

EGYPT

Growing up out of the river

Out of the dark brown mud of an African rain

Growing up out of the river

Swimming in the centuries

Black Athena of the ancient world

Dancing in the triangle and the square

Pythagoras and astronomy

Moses and Deuteronomy

Papyrus and the hieroglyph

Tempting Plato to leave his cave

And question the universe

Swept over by the Hyksos,

Romans and Mohammedans

Christians and Napoleons, British

And the never ending battle

Of wind and river, sand and mud

Mother of the Mediterranean

The Red Sea, and the Aegean,

Bowed down under the centuries

The brown top of Africa

Surrounded by a new black mud

That is drowning Arabia in a sea of blood

And the wind beings rise up

Desert wind sweeping the continents

Shivering the spider web world of

Sky and Fox, BBC, Al Jazeera

Listen to the children

Growing up out of the river

Where the Nile delta sings

In the cotton field spring

In the spinning wheel whine

In the factory roar

In the millions who pour into Tahrir square

Chanting *"Baoo demana we Baoo Kalaweena"*

You have stolen our blood and kidneys

"We Bneshhat Ehna we Ahaleena"

We are the starving families

You have given our land to strangers

You have traded in lies and torture

You have dined on blood and murder

You live in palaces

Drive by us in limousines

Fly over us in jets

Rule over us as if we were nothing but slaves

Now we rise up from the grave

And you will do anything to stop us

Ballot boxes stuffed full of corpses

Rape and religion wedded to make monsters

And yes, you can kill us in millions

But how will you live then

Who will feed you

Who will dig your wells of water and oil

Who will build your chariots and palaces

Who will build your magnificent tombs

You will never defeat us

We carry the earth on our backs

We open our mouths and speak in flame

We lift up our eyes and see it is you who are afraid

We will bury you

And your bones will nourish our dreams

BULLET

(London, August 2011)

Bang! out of the barrel of a gun I sped

Into the body of a black man

Into the body of a black

BOY BOY BOY

Assume the position

Spread 'em wide

In front of your girl friend

In front of your mother

In front of your daughter and son

Put you in prison, yes, and I kill plenty

But even better, I make you into your own death penalty

I am the *War On Terror*. You are the enemy within

Man or woman, high or low.

Don't bother to show me your diploma

It's there on your skin

You are the flame of resistance

That I can never quite extinguish

You are the angry fire that I fear more

Than truth, and I am the definition of liar

You are the light that blazed up in Tottenham
And a hundred other places, so bright
It could be seen across the Mediterranean
I am the darkness waiting
You are the stand-up-straight of a new generation.
You are the broken glass and torn up pavement
You are the golden beach beneath, if only you can find it
I am the man on the TV calling you mindless

I watch you
Change into every color and race
Communicate in ways I can't keep up with
Be brave a thousand times in every hour
But look around – I still have power

I am the bullet and the gun. I am the serpent tongue
I move armies, empty bellies, turn bones to dust
I am a treasure chest of fantasy, pleasure and shame
I have access to your brain more often than you do
I'm running with you on your feet, it's my arm too
That torched your neighbour's shop, my fingers you
Must free from an iron grip around your thoughts
Kettling you, ghetto-ing you, four long days and nights
Letting you burn the wrong places, keeping you out of the right
Revolution is a hurricane and the wind blows wildly
When young lions roar in pain and strike out blindly
Jackals hide in the tall grass waiting their chance
Until you learn to fight with wisdom, I rule the dance

DUH-MOCKRACY

Back in the Middle Ages

They had this thing called

The Church

And it was their gig to tell you God's will and what to do about it

Then Martin Luther hit the nail on the head and said

You decide

But that was too simple and way too dangerous

So they backed off, made a few changes

And came up with this thing called

    Duh-mockracy!

Who decides

    Duh-mockracy!

Where God is the man with the TV stations

God is the man with the guns to take 'em

God is the man with the money to buy the guns to take the stations to con-

Vince the nation that he is the suppository of divine revelation

Who decides

    Well, we all took a vote and I voted against it, but...

Who decides

    Well, I don't like it but there's nothin' I can do about it...

Who put the lines on the maps that make the corpses fall on one side

While the other side plays

Duh-mockracy!

Who drew the lines around Palestine

Who dug a ditch around an oil field and called it Kuwait

They say there are no pacifists in gasoline lines, but

When the majority votes for national salvation

When the majority votes for mass incineration

When the majority votes for racial purification

Fuck 'em

THE AGE OF ENLIGHTENMENT

Je m'appelle Denis Diderot

They sentenced me to twenty-one years
Of frequent hunger and constant hard work
I thanked the judges and rolled up my sleeves
We were building a dictionary of the world
Covering everything related to human curiosity
So naturally we began sniffing at the asshole of the universe
Where the most beautiful flowers grow in shit
The sweet smell of stink, the love of calluses, rough hands
Dumb pleasures, howls of pain, life hungry death
Filth and excess, the word made flesh, and yet
Glowing inside, like a morning sunrise –
The rational mind

We collected everything, studied the work of every hand, documented every
skill, engaged the great minds of our continent, cast it all into movable type,
fired up printing presses day and night, shipped out books by the wagon
load, trailing mule shit and wheel ruts, crossing mountains, dodging floods.
We were an industry of the mind, making a new kind of product, selling it
to all kinds of people – not only priests and scholars – they drank us down
in the tea and coffee houses, and when they opened their mouths, our
words came out, but in a new blend, with the flavour of each new mind,

and it bubbled over into the streets and alleys, palaces and dives, even just talking was intoxicating, as we all drank down the spirit of the times.

How could we be to blame for the holocaust to come, when we were fighting for the magic of the mind's wonders, for the freedom to ask any question? We were not an infection, not fanatics – we were the enemy of everything dogmatic – and revolution was not a religion, it was a clap of thunder, it was a prison break over the crumbling walls of a dying empire out into the wide open space. We were the liberators of the human race. How could we be to blame for napalm and the atom bomb, slavery, genocide, and a planet ripped wide open and gutted for profit and pleasure.

TIME OUT FOR DIALECTICS

We live in a metaphysical age
Physical, because even the invisible is material
Matter in motion, an infinite ocean of repetition and change
Meta-physical, because we never see it the way it is
We see it the way we make it to be
Which isn't to say it's make-believe
It's make-happen
And the happening is how we see
Until it becomes a habit and then it becomes how we don't see
Don't see the new
Don't even see the possibility of the new
But one divides into two
That's dialectics

For example…

May I borrow your chair?

Metaphysics says – the chair is there

I know it's there, because when I sit on it

(sits on it)

My ass doesn't hit the floor

Metaphysics says – the chair is there

Dialectics says – yes, it is there

On the other hand

(kicks chair across stage)

No it fucking isn't!

Everything divides into two

Because everything is coming and going

Atoms, electrons, ideas, emotions

Never entirely here or there but always kind of on the way

We look out at the world and see objects floating in space

But there is no truly empty space, and no absolutely indivisible object

Everything is process, movement and storm

One divides into two

The old and the new

The dying away and the fighting to be born

That's dialectics

BACK TO THE ENLIGHTENMENT

We were born into a world of circles, tied up in tradition, bowed down in obligation to those who stood outside, above our circle, who were only ever in a higher circle. I bow to you, you bow to him, he bows to the lord, the lord bows to the king, and we all bow down to god or the devil, it doesn't really matter which, because even hell is in circles.

And in a world like this, property was kind of democratic
Because it wasn't truly property until it could be taken away
By anybody – from anybody – the democracy of money

Property was individuality
Property broke down borders
Property was the atomic one
Multiplied by infinity
Property was possibility
Without property, there was no trade
No travel from country to country
Without property, there was no geography

And when we found that the products of the mind could be turned into
property
Peasants who played violins for the lord and lady's pleasure
Became composers, makers of sheets of music that could be bought and
sold
Even ideas became a new kind of gold
And what could you buy with it?
Freedom
The freedom of things
In the marketplace of ideas

There are those who argue
That true science and philosophy
Began with money

That the idea of a universal substance

Was not simply dreamed up

It was invented

Money became a fact

Then it became an idea

Only then did we ask

If anything can be measured in money

What is it that money measures

And so it began

The search for a universal glue

That would bind us together

But one divides into two

And if money is the measure

It must also be true

That anything can be broken into pieces

And counted

As property

Books

Property

Ideas

Property

Cows

Property

Loaves of bread

Property

Men

Property

Women

Property

We should have known

If anything can be measured in money

Property isn't ownership

It's being owned

BEAST MARKET

(Capital, chapters 1-4)

The Beast speaks

If I were alive

I would be your greatest lover

I would build you cities, feed your children

Fill up your lives with music and dancing

I would cover the earth with wheat fields and rice paddies

Drill down into its core to pull out strings of steel and oil

I would scrape the sky with desert sand melted into glass

Cool the hot, heat the cold, charm the fish out of the oceans

And teach the trees to stand in a row and rain down manna

I would multiply you

If I were alive

I would teach you the meaning of hell

I would blast you with war, rip your children from your arms

Swallow them in famine, smother them into silence

Dry up their tears with death

I would teach you to fear your neighbor

Train you to march in step

You might even come to believe in me

Isn't this how a wounded god would love?

With kindness and gifts, wonderful gifts

Mixed in with pieces of heartless cruelty

And if my cruelty is on a global scale

So are my gifts

And the greatest gift of all, I would do this through you

How else could it be? You made me. Now I make you

I am the law of value

The profit and loss ledger of the earth

I was born in the gulf between what you can do

And what you are worth

And look around

You can do miracles

But what are you worth...

How much do you eat

Do you live in a house or on the street

What does it take to make and replace you

That much, no one can take away from you

And still leave you

But after that, everything is fair game

After that, it becomes worthwhile to own a slave

After that, the more you make, the more there is to steal

Until you, who produce the food, become the meal

And the wonders you have made

Become a curse, become a plague

Become a gang of howling wolves

But somehow they are riding in sleighs

And it's you all pulling at the traces

And the whip cracks – that's me – I am the whip
But the wolves imagine they are in control and they
Snarl and slash at each other as they drive you forward
And you do go forward
So what if you leave behind a trail of blood

I am the hurricane that blows you through life
The profit drive, the whip of the world
I am measured in money but I am not money
I am in every good that goes to market but I am not physical
I am in every tool but I am not useful
I am you, your sweat, your time, your mind
Stolen away from you and congealed into a ghost
Not an evil spirit but an abstract principle
Coded into the grooves of habit and material
I weigh the world and say what is valuable
What counts
And it happens
Over an almost infinite number of individual transactions
I swallow and digest every exception, I break all regulation
I am the price of everything, I am the universal religion
I am the law
I am God
Kill me
Or I will own you forever

SANTA

Imagine you were this cool old guy who loved children

Truly and deeply

Loved every beat of the way they stiff-little-tick-tock walk, and the monkey talk, and the roar of the buzz of the whisper of the butterfly why of honey and wonder and thirsty hunger. They give you their hand with everything in it, and your heart lurches into… Give me a place to stand and I will move the universe, squeeze it down into the perfect toy to light the smile inside your… I… would give you anything. Imagine this, multiplied by every newborn smile in a heartbreak world – if you could be *Santa* for every boy and girl. Imagine a magic workshop powered by twinkle of the eye drive, quantum indecision, and reindeer jive, every elf in all eleven dimensions, drugged and demented, but working with manic precision, a just-in-the-nick-of-time engine (that's why they call you Saint Nick), and in the back of the sleigh a bag big enough to carry its weight in wishes – this is it! the delicious impossible minute when every child on the planet is given the one perfect gift that says this is your world – and you belong in it

Imagine you could do this one wonderful thing

But for the rest of the year that was all you could do

And the toys would go out and be used up and worn out and broken

And that was good, the way it should be, that was why you would build them

Toys were made to be broken, not children

But in the war-torn days of the in-between year, the names would change
but it was always King Herod's reign, and his soldiers would go from door
to door with bloody swords, while you all worked on through tears and
horror, knowing you could never make it right, no matter how magical that
one

perfect

night

What would you do?

Would you go on working

When you could only give the one magic minute

Better than nothing, and who could argue with arithmetic

Or would you go crazy with the weight of anger and grief

Would you feel responsible, would you feel like a thief

Living a life so sweet, full of hard work done well

When so many children are living in hell

Some people can't ever get enough

Give them a minute and they want eternity, the kind who can never be
happy with even a scrap of cruelty, they go crazy at the thought of one child
dying a needless death, they can't rest, they've got to be moving, doing,
making more than a difference, making EVERYTHING different

These are the Crazy Santas who never give up

Crazy Santas mad with love

Crazy Santas get up at the crack of dawn, work boots on, march out onto
the field, into the street, get beat, fight back, get shot at, don't stop, live life
hot-wired

Crazy Santas are dangerous, but it's a dangerous world

Some people can't help fighting back whenever they see the weak attacked

They live like champions in the army of the never-had-a-chance

Some of them pick up the gun

Some of them live like saints

All of them are powered by love

All of them make mistakes

Some say we need more magic minutes that's the best we can do

But I believe we need to reach out for eternity we need to be

Crazy Santas who never give up

Crazy Santas mad with love

SAMSON

Did you ever wish you could be like Samson

Hair grown long again

Big and strong again

Between the pillars of

Right and wrong again

One mighty shove and then

Bring it all tumbling down

The end of a nightmare world

Where baby girls are put to death

For the crime of being the wrong sex

Where girls and boys are given guns instead of toys

And made to fight and die for the light

That's stolen from their eyes, cut to fit

And pasted on a Wall Street banker's diamond tie clip

Yeah, maybe the whip and the African slave ship

Have been replaced by the ticker tape and the microchip

And the factory sweatshop has sprouted legs

And learned to walk across borders

But every new world order it's the same old song

Where the rich have rights and the poor get wronged

And the chairman of the board and the drug lord

And the gun dealer and the born again politician faith healer

They're all singing in the same choir

Swinging and swaying at the same club

You get baptized in fire

They get their sins washed away

In oil and money and blood

Did you ever feel like Noah before the flood

Praying for the day some vengeful god

Would say – I've had enough

And wash those bastards away

Did you ever feel like Hercules

Sent out to slay the many-headed beast

But every time you chop off one head

Whack!

Two more grow back

Did you ever feel like you had so much love locked up inside

But you couldn't let it out, couldn't let it go

Had to keep hold of an icy cold silence

Or you might explode in mindless, raging violence

Living in a Marvel Comic Book strip

Knowing that the planet's in a death grip

Looking for a power that can shake it

Looking for a weapon that can break it

Look at all the love you got inside you

Let it be the fire that ignites you

Living in a world of violence

But the power is love and the weapon is…

Science…

Is dangerous, it

Brings on changes, and it

Opens up possibilities

Even the ground beneath our feet is

Not so solid, not so safe

They burned scientists at the stake

'Cause they were afraid of the trouble we'd make

And you know what? They were right

We can make day from night

We can turn darkness into light

And the power that reaches out to the stars

And into the atom and back in time

Can turn on a dime

And look at the lock on the prison bars

That keep us caged

It's a power that grows from age to age

From the work of the hand and the work of the brain

We think and we do and we dream and we make

And we learn from the lesson of every mistake

And all our achievements and all that is known

Are built on the bones of what's come before

It's true of the study of stones, stars, biology and human society

So when the powers that be sneer at our history

At our victory and defeat in the laboratory of the street

They not only steal from the living, they rob the dead

Of all that they fought and bled and died for

From the back alleys of Paris to the storming of the Winter Palace

From the cane fields of Haiti to the Vietnam rice paddy

From Tiananmen to Tahrir Square

From Malcolm to Marx, Mau Mau to Chairman Mao

These are our bones, our stepping stones to tomorrow

And the modern day vampires try to suck out the marrow

Of knowledge and vision and the courage that comes with them

But you who are fighting for a world that's not bought and sold

Where only in the human heart do you find the truest gold

You must be warriors with heads that are old

With wisdom and young with fire

Oh my sisters, oh my brothers

Don't believe the liars

WHAT IS TO BE DONE

the revolution will not come until it has pierced your heart

until every cruelty and injustice
no matter who it is done to
feels as if it were done to you
until you are naked, open wide
wounded by every homeless cry
a mother to every hungry child
a native son to every tribe
stranded in the forest flame
swallowing smoke and tears of rage
running from the thunder of a helicopter gun
the revolution will not come

until your back aches
and the sun bakes you
and the pain breaks you
until every minute of your life hurts
and the ripe fruit falls down into the dirt
because your fingers and your bones and your brain are numb
the revolution will not come

until every cop car is looking for you
for what you are, not what you do
and you stand on the earth, branded
by the wrong accent, the wrong colour skin
the wrong sexuality, the wrong mother tongue
too fat, too thin, too old, too young
the revolution will not come

until you walk the street, bearing unwanted seed
condemned to breed by men who call you girl
and think they fucking own the world
until you stare up into the hate-filled face of a rapist thrusting into you
when you can smell his breath, taste the rancid kiss
when your stomach twists in anger and disgust
when you can feel all this as if it were done to you
 – it's not enough

because the revolution will not come until it has made you wise

so what if you hate injustice
so what if you're willing to die to make a change
it's not enough to be brave, not even enough to love
unless love leads to wisdom, when push comes to shove

so you learn to read books and faces
you study what gender and race is
you look at science and the economy
at every class and group in society
you study the past but you don't live in it – you don't worship it
you don't pick through the rubble for a lost god to believe in
you read history not with a branding iron, but a blowtorch
you are not a king, you are not a priest
you are not singing in the fucking choir
you are the fire that burns through history
your genealogy is written in the ashes of
burnt-out villages, crucified slaves
weavers, chained to their looms
heretics, burned at the stake
screaming out the truth

how many thousands of years of fighting
each other over the never-enough, one
class after another rising to the top and
beating back down everyone else with
laws and religion and bullets when you don't listen
how many thousands of years of system after system

and always the same fundamental division

you work, they rule

but you are more than just a talking tool

let the revolution be your school

study the connections

and you begin to see the chains of slavery

are chains of power too

they connect you

to an army of the dispossessed

and it's an army you will need

because the revolution will not come until it has made you strong

power is a good thing
try living without it
but without a doubt it divides into two
the power to win is the power to lose
power is nothing but the power to choose
it's only as good as how you use it

but never forget
you are not begging for mercy
you are fighting for power

how will you break free of the ingrained habits of a lifetime
how will you gain control of your own minds
how will you bring it together to set off a chain reaction
and if you win
how will you fight off the armies that come to crush you
and if you win
how will you feed the world
and if you win
how will you carry through –
how will you free the world

be leaders who know how to be led
be teachers who know how to be taught
revolution is war – it has to be fought
they've got the guns and the weapons of mass communication
you've got the power to the people that comes with organization

you've got the power to the people
but you better believe they hate it
if you give 'em a chance they'll break it
you know it's only as good as you make it
you've got the power to the people
are you ready to take it

ABOUT THE AUTHOR

David Lee Morgan has travelled the world as a performance poet and street musician (saxophone). He has won many poetry slams, including the London and U.K. Slam Championships. He is a longstanding member of the Writers Guild and holds a PhD in Creative Writing from Newcastle University. He lives in London, grew up in the U.S., was born in Berlin and considers himself a citizen of the planet.